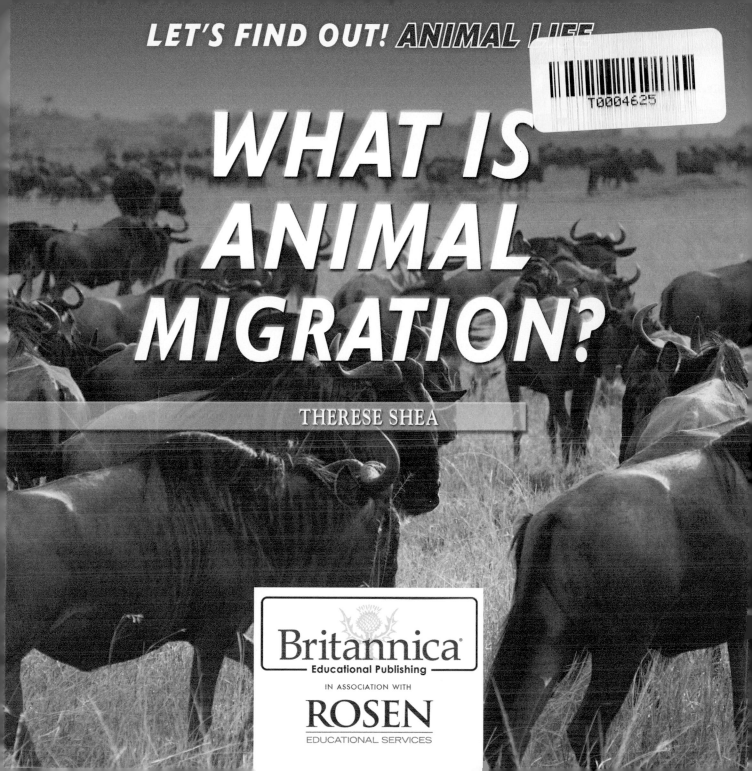

WHAT IS ANIMAL MIGRATION?

THERESE SHEA

Britannica®
Educational Publishing

IN ASSOCIATION WITH

ROSEN
EDUCATIONAL SERVICES

T0004625

Published in 2016 by Britannica Educational Publishing (a trademark of Encyclopædia Britannica, Inc.) in association with The Rosen Publishing Group, Inc.
29 East 21st Street, New York, NY 10010

Distributed exclusively by Rosen Publishing.
To see additional Britannica Educational Publishing titles, go to rosenpublishing.com.

First Edition

<u>Britannica Educational Publishing</u>
J. E. Luebering: Director, Core Reference Group
Mary Rose McCudden: Editor, Britannica Student Encyclopedia

<u>Rosen Publishing</u>
Hope Lourie Killcoyne: Executive Editor
Shalini Saxena: Editor
Nelson Sá: Art Director
Brian Garvey: Designer
Cindy Reiman: Photography Manager
Sherri Jackson: Photo Researcher

Library of Congress Cataloging-in-Publication Data

Shea, Therese.
What is animal migration?/Therese Shea.
        pages cm. — (Let's find out! Animal life)
Includes bibliographical references and index.
ISBN 978-1-68048-010-8 (library bound) — ISBN 978-1-68048-011-5 (pbk.) — ISBN 978-1-68048-013-9 (6-pack)
1. Animal migration—Juvenile literature. I. Title.
QL754.S54 2014
591.56'8—dc23

2014037715

Manufactured in the United States of America

Cover, p. 1 Ann Manner/Photodisc/Getty Images; pp. 4–5 Jacynthroode/iStock/Thinkstock; p. 5 © McDonald Wildlife Photography/Animals Animals; p. 6–7 justasc/Shutterstock.com; p. 7 © McPHOTO/E. u. H. Pum/age fotostock; pp. 8, 12 Encyclopædia Britannica, Inc.; p. 9 Jimmyhuynh/iStock/Thinkstock; p. 10 Kris Davidson/Lonely Planet Images/Getty Images; p. 11 Arendvdwalt/iStock/Thinkstock; pp. 12–13 Jeff Mondragon/age fotostock/SuperStock; p. 14 © Michael Francis Photography/Animals Animals; p. 15 © Santiago Urquijo/Moment/Getty Images; p. 16 Ardea/Fink, Kenneth/Animals Animals; p. 17 Sarun T/Shutterstock.com; p. 18 Datacraft Co Ltd/Getty Images; p. 19 Tom Lynn/Aurora/Getty Images; p. 20 Gillardi Jacques/hemis.fr/Getty Images; p. 21 Fred Bruemmer/Photolibrary/Getty Images; p. 22 © D Maehrmann/age fotostock; p. 23 Elena Tyapkina/iStock/Thinkstock; p. 24 Artie Raslich/Getty Images; p. 25 © Martin Woike/age fotostock; p. 26 © Zoonar/gero b/age fotostock; p. 27 © Mariola Bednar/age fotostock; p. 28 Juniors/SuperStock; p. 29 Peter Lillie/ Gallo Images/Getty Images; interior pages background image Oleg Znamenskiy/Shutterstock.com.

CONTENTS

TIME TO TRAVEL

Many people take trips each year in search of good weather and good food. So do animals. These traveling creatures are called migrants, and their trips are called migrations. Many animals migrate to find food or to reproduce. Others migrate to find better weather.

Most kinds of migrant animals make a round trip each year. Grazing animals follow seasonal changes. They look for green plants to eat. Some fish

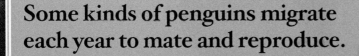

Some kinds of penguins migrate each year to mate and reproduce.

COMPARE AND CONTRAST
Some animals move from one place to another and stay there. They do not return to the starting place. Migrating animals make the return trip. Can you think of animals that move only one way?

African elephants, such as these, migrate across land each year in large numbers in order to find food and water.

and sea creatures move according to the seasons for different reasons.

Many animals make long journeys back and forth across land and ocean or through the air. Other migrations are vertical, such as up or down a mountain. Either way, migrations are not vacations for animals. They are important, often life-saving, journeys.

Winging It

Perhaps the best-known migrant animals are birds. More than a third of all bird species migrate. Many birds migrate in large groups. These include birds that usually like to live alone, such as birds of prey. Many flocks of birds, like geese or ducks, form a V shape when they migrate. The V shape helps the birds save energy as they fly. The birds behind the leader do not have to work as hard

VOCABULARY

A **species** is a certain type, or kind, of animal or plant.

Some birds like to fly in a certain spot in the V shape. Others take turns being the leader.

These Arctic terns fly above the Arctic Ocean near Norway. Arctic terns have the longest migration of any bird.

as the leader does. They are pulled along by the air flowing over the leader. The birds take turns being the leader so they can all keep flying longer.

Small and large birds may cross as many as 1,000 miles (1,600 kilometers) of land and water. Some trips are even longer. The arctic tern travels about 22,000 miles (35,000 km) as it flies between the Arctic and Antarctica!

Birds migrate mostly to find places with more food or good sites where they can nest. In some species, male birds migrate first to choose a nesting site. In other cases, males

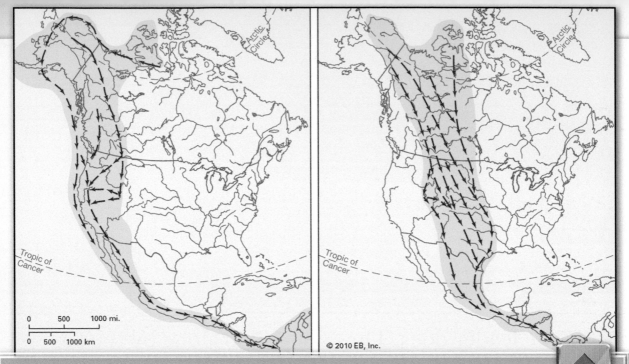

These maps show two migration routes that many species of birds use: the Pacific Flyway (*left*) and the Central Flyway (*right*).

and females choose their mates along the way. Geese, which mate for life, travel as couples in large flocks.

Small inland birds and shorebirds fly by night and feed by day. Other birds are daytime travelers. Many small birds fly at low altitude during the day, about 200 feet (61 meters) above the ground. Some birds fly much higher. In northwestern India, geese have been seen at altitudes

Many hummingbird species spend the winter in Central America and Mexico. Some don't migrate at all, however.

of 30,000 feet (9,100 meters).

Not all birds migrate. Even birds of the same species may not all migrate, depending on where they live. For example, many birds are migratory in northern and eastern Europe, while similar species in western Europe are more likely to stay close to home.

THINK ABOUT IT

Tall buildings, such as skyscrapers and lighthouses, can be dangers to migrating birds. The birds can hurt or even kill themselves by flying into these buildings. What can people do to make areas more bird friendly?

Huge Herds

Few land animals migrate. This is because walking is slow and can take a lot of time and energy. However, in some areas, plants grow only in certain seasons of the year. Animals may have to migrate to different areas to graze. In the Arctic, caribou (reindeer) settle during the summer in treeless, grassy plains. Then, the herds move south and

Large herds of caribou often migrate farther than smaller groups. They are safer from animal attacks in larger numbers.

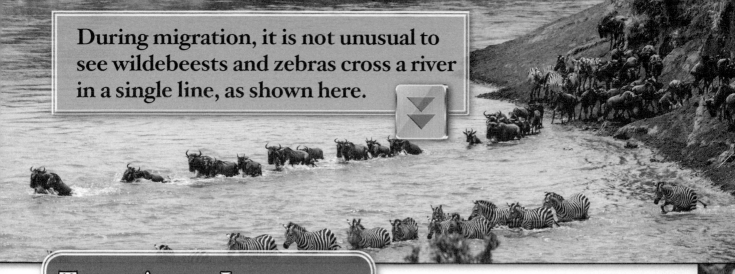

During migration, it is not unusual to see wildebeests and zebras cross a river in a single line, as shown here.

THINK ABOUT IT

No meat-eating animals migrate. However, wolves sometimes follow migrating herds of caribou. Why do you think this is?

spend the winter looking for plants to eat in forests. In early spring, the caribou travel north again. This is the longest migration in North America.

Large African mammals migrate with the wet and dry seasons. Zebras, wildebeests, and other plains animals travel more than 1,000 miles (1,600 km) through Tanzania. During the rains, herds spread out. During the dry season, they gather around watering holes. Elephants, too, wander great distances in search of food and water.

Marine Migrations

Some sea, or marine, mammals also migrate. Gray whales have the longest known migration of any mammal. They may travel 12,000 miles (19,300 km) round trip every year. They give birth in the warm waters of Mexico in winter. This is because their babies, called calves, don't have enough body fat to live in cold waters. Then, the whales go to the Arctic to feed in the summer.

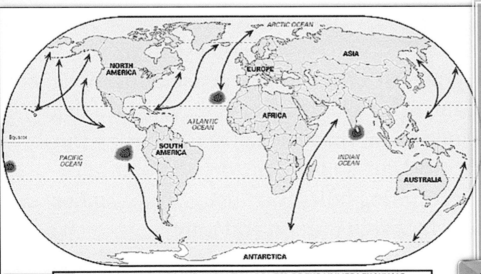

BREEDING GROUNDS AND MIGRATION ROUTES OF THE HUMPBACK WHALE
- Breeding Grounds
- Migration Routes

This world map shows that humpback whales mate and give birth in warmer waters. They then return to colder waters.

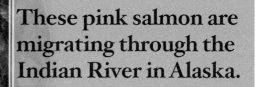

These pink salmon are migrating through the Indian River in Alaska.

Many fish migrate each year. Eggs and young fish drift with the current, but adults usually swim against the current toward their breeding grounds.

Salmon lay their eggs in rivers, in freshwater. When the fish hatch, they swim down the river to the oceans where they will live. When it is time to lay their own eggs, the fish return to the same river in which they were born to lay their eggs in freshwater. Some swim more than 1,850 miles (3,000 km). Some fish die after this trip. Others make the same journey year after year.

COMPARE AND CONTRAST
Compare and contrast the journeys of gray whales and salmon. What do they do to help their offspring survive?

Up and Down

The most famous migrations are horizontal, or across water, land, or air. However, other animal migrations are vertical, or up and down. Elk, bighorn sheep, mule deer, and some bird species live high up in the mountains in the summer but move to lower elevations in winter. Higher elevations receive more snow and colder weather in the winter. So these animals can more easily find plants to eat at lower elevations.

Elk in Theodore Roosevelt National Park in North Dakota climb to higher elevations in summer.

Earthworms return to the surface in warmer weather—just in time for spring birds to eat!

Some earthworms move from the top of the soil in warmer weather to deeper underground in the winter. If they didn't do this, they would freeze.

Many sea creatures remain deep underwater during the day and rise to the surface at night. Zooplankton are tiny animals. Scientists guess zooplankton feed on other plankton at the surface at night and return to deeper waters during the day to avoid predators.

> **VOCABULARY**
> **Predators** are animals that hunt, kill, and eat other animals to survive.

TURN RIGHT AT THE RIVER?

Migrating animals have no maps to guide them. But they still find their way over long distances. Some animals use land features such as rivers and mountains to tell where they are. Birds have been seen "exploring" as they search for landmarks. Even whales and fish use underwater landforms as clues.

Migrating sandhill crane flocks fly very high and often use landmarks such as mountains as clues to guide them on their routes.

THINK ABOUT IT

Scientists think that birds use many different landmarks during their migration. What do you think happens if one of the landmarks they use changes?

Many birds have a built-in sense of direction. They are able to fly in a certain direction over a long period of time. They can also tell which direction to go in order to get home.

Young birds that do not migrate with their parents seem to know the direction in which they should go but do not know exactly where to land. However, after they find a place to spend the winter, they will return to the same place again and again.

Some bat species sleep through winter, while others migrate. Bats that migrate use some of their senses as well as the Sun to find their destination.

Using the Sky

Birds that fly during the day use the Sun to find the right direction. Fish, too, use objects in the sky to find their way. However, the Sun's position is much harder to find as its rays pass through water.

Birds that fly at night may be guided by patterns of stars. This even works indoors! When an image of the night sky is on the ceiling, like in

Birds may use certain stars and star patterns to figure out direction.

Whooping cranes have died out in much of the United States. Scientists are trying to help the remaining birds survive. One way they are helping is by using small airplanes to teach the birds how to migrate. Do you think this will work?

A scientist uses a whooping crane puppet to feed a young bird.

a planetarium, birds can figure out where to go. When clouds are present and the Sun and stars cannot be seen, birds can use wind patterns as a guide.

SUPER SENSES

It is possible that many migrating animals use several senses at once in their travels. Migrating salmon are drawn by the odor, or smell, of the waters of the river where they

THINK ABOUT IT

Some migrating birds do not stop to eat during migration. They keep flying. Why do you think this is?

Even though Christmas Island red crabs do not stay with their young, red crabs know how to migrate from the shore to the sea and back each year.

lived when they were young. Wildebeests may be able to smell rain from far away and use this sense to direct their migration route.

Scientists have decided that some animals must be born knowing how to find their way. Their parents pass this knowledge on to them. Scientists think this is the only way they can know where certain places are.

Wildebeests in Kenya follow the rain to find rich grasslands such as this.

Scientists think migrating honeybees use their magnetic sense in combination with their memory of landmarks.

Another great help to migration is a magnetic sense. Some birds, fish, and even honeybees are thought to migrate by using Earth's magnetic field. Scientists have found magnetic-sensitive cells in the bodies of trout that may help them navigate.

After baby loggerhead sea turtles hatch on beaches, they crawl into the Atlantic Ocean to start a migration

8,000 miles (13,000 km) long. Scientists think these reptiles are born with a "magnetic map." When they come upon changes in Earth's magnetic field, they change direction. Baby loggerhead turtles in scientists' tanks changed directions when exposed to certain magnetic fields, too.

> **VOCABULARY**
>
> A **magnetic field** is the space near a magnet in which its magnetic forces can be felt. Earth acts as a giant magnet because it has iron and other metals at its center.

Baby loggerhead turtles must enter the water quickly after hatching. They are easy prey for predators on the beach.

PACKING FOR THE TRIP

How do animals know when to migrate? There is usually something in the environment that signals that it is time to leave. For example, there might be a drop in temperature, less food available, or a change in the amount of sunlight. Then, an animal's brain cues its body to start preparing for the trip. Many animals, such as birds and whales, eat a lot more before they travel because a long migration takes a huge amount of energy.

A humpback whale finds a school of fish to snack on. Fish and other food provide migrating whales with the energy they need to travel.

Animals that hibernate for the winter prepare their bodies by eating a lot. Then they stay in one place for the rest of winter. They don't eat, and they barely breathe. How are hibernation and migration similar? How are they different?

For example, the bar-tailed godwit bird eats so much before migration that it doubles its weight. During its flight, it loses a lot of this weight. Similar changes have been seen in other migrating birds. These changes do not happen in animals that do not migrate, however.

Bar-tailed godwits breed in the Arctic and other cold areas but spend winters in warmer areas, like Australia and New Zealand.

ALL IN THE FAMILY

Some species of insects migrate over more than one generation. This means it takes longer than the lifetime of any one insect to reach the destination and return. The painted lady butterfly takes six generations to complete a round trip between Africa and the Arctic. Each individual butterfly makes it only part of the way on the 9,000-mile (14,484 km) trip.

The painted lady butterfly lives only about two weeks.

Dragonflies need freshwater to breed. During their migration, they stop in areas where this is plentiful.

Some species of dragonflies have an even longer migration. The globe skimmer dragonfly may travel as many as 11,000 miles (17,700 kilometers) over four generations. Scientists think the dragonflies follow wind patterns as they migrate between Africa and India. This is the longest known insect migration.

Scientists have not discovered how a generation knows where to go in its migration path. Each individual is not following its parents or remembering a route it traveled before. It is likely that the dragonflies are born with a sense that tells them where to go.

MIGRATION MEANS SURVIVAL

Migration helps animals survive. If they didn't migrate, many animals would die of cold or lack of food. Species might die out because they do not have a safe place to reproduce.

However, the world is changing, and these changes can affect migrating animals. In southern Africa,

Most walrus species migrate north in the summer and south in the winter. Mothers need sea ice to give birth.

A herd of springbok runs at full speed in the African country of Botswana.

COMPARE AND CONTRAST

It's harder for people to keep land migration routes open than routes in the sky. Why do you think this is?

hundreds of thousands of springbok, a type of antelope, once migrated in huge herds. There were so many of them that any animal in the way was either swept along with the herd or trampled! However, people built many fences, roads, farms, and buildings in their path. By the late 1800s, the springbok were no longer able to migrate.

Today, scientists are working to make sure other migration routes remain open so the animals can continue their amazing journeys. Their lives depend on it!

GLOSSARY

altitude The height of something above the level of the sea.

breed To produce young animals.

destination A place to which one is traveling.

environment The conditions that surround something and affect growth and health.

grazing Feeding on plants.

hibernate To pass the winter in a resting state.

insects Small animals that have six legs and a body formed of three parts.

journey The act of traveling from one place to another.

landmark A usually large object on land that is easy to see and can help someone or something find the way to a place near it.

mammals Animals that produce live young, feed their young milk, and have hair or fur on their bodies.

mate To come together to breed; one of a pair of animals that come together to breed.

navigate To find the way to get to a place.

offspring The young of an animal or plant.

planetarium A building or room in which images of stars, planets, and other heavenly bodies are shown on a high, curved ceiling.

reproduce To breed; to have offspring, or children.

route A course that people or animals travel.

seasonal Occurring or growing only in a certain season or seasons.

trample Walk or step heavily on something so as to cause pain or injury.

For More Information

Books

Berkes, Marianne Collins. *Going Home: The Mystery of Animal Migration*. Nevada City, CA: Dawn Publications, 2010.

Cooper, Sharon Katz. *When Whales Cross the Sea: The Gray Whale Migration*. North Mankato, MN: Picture Window Books, 2015.

Hirsch, Rebecca E. *Arctic Tern Migration*. Mankato, MN: Child's World, 2012.

Kant, Tanya. *The Migration of a Butterfly*. New York, NY: Children's Press, 2009.

Mcbane, Jeanie. *Animal Migration*. North Mankato, MN: Capstone Press, 2013.

Nelson, Robin. *Migration*. Minneapolis, MN: Lerner, 2011.

Websites

Because of the changing nature of Internet links, Rosen Publishing has developed an online list of websites related to the subject of this book. This site is updated regularly. Please use this link to access this list:

http://www.rosenlinks.com/LFO/Migr

INDEX